DEDICATION

For my beautiful ancestors Doris Daley, Mary Fenton and Josephine Fenton.

DEAR
ANCESTORS

poems & reflections on the African diaspora

CP PATRICK

Field Order Press
718 7th St NW, Washington, DC 20001
www.fieldorderpress.com

Publisher's Note: Names, characters, places, and incidents are a product of the author's imagination. Locales and public names are sometimes used for atmospheric purposes. Any resemblance to actual people, living or dead, or to businesses, companies, events, institutions, or locales is completely coincidental.

Cover Illustration © 2016 Damonza

Dear Ancestors/CP Patrick. -- 1st ed.
ISBN-13 978-0692598429

DEAR
ANCESTORS

CONTENTS

BONDAGE

FREEDOM OR SOMETHING LIKE IT

ABOUT THE AUTHOR

HOME

we were
once
sunshine
laughter
free
not black nor brown
dark nor fair
we simply were
happy

| once

yellow sun
sky bright blue
bowls with yams
pots of stew
father's wisdom
mother's care
family to laugh with
friends to dare
earth below
sky above
all we needed
to feel loved

| home

it was always there
dark bodies danced
warriors fought
anything to taste
sweetness
large hands
caressed thick curves
full lips whispered promises
soft brown skin against soft brown skin
magic
pulled love
between thighs
and into hearts

| the original magic

we
loved
kissed
prayed
your belly swelled
i was not a man
until i took you for my wife

| marriage

you heard beasts were coming
did you believe such things
of boats that could not sink
no matter how many of your people went inside
or did you say
no one would do such things
even then
you trusted
until shown
the truth

| trust issues

you valued
love
land
and your ancestors' bones

|worth

brown eyes
dark curls
long neck
ebony shoulders
i watched
until
i could no longer see
pieces of you
what life would we have lived
you were
mine
until
they stole
my dreams

| abducted

here is a name you may not know
nzinga mbemba ruled the kongo years ago
wealthy and cunning
a brilliant mind
but like so many
too trusting, too kind
mbemba's people were kidnapped and sold
black bodies
worth more than diamonds and gold

| 1526

they say
you sold your brothers and sisters
you too are guilty
but your minds could not imagine
horror awaited
those you bartered
i say
you would have never sold another
even your enemies
if you only knew

| you are not guilty

red mouths pleaded
brown eyes cried
your captors were not convinced
pretending they could not hear
refusing to acknowledge
mothers and fathers
daughters and sons

| humans

they did not leave your birthplace empty-handed
attached to chains
bound ankles and wrists
were hearts

| Africa

MIDDLE PASSAGE
SECOND HOME

when your feet were forced
your walk more stumbles than steps
and you smelled salt in the air
the first time
you went aboard the slave ship
scorching skin
branded with hot iron
did you know
the fight within your blood
would live for generations

| questions

we envision
boats with white sails
calm blue waters
against serene bright skies
but it was dark
all of it
dark

| in the belly of the beast

men
kings and princes
craftsmen and farmers
warriors and healers
some were
emasculated
weeping souls
unable to defend their families
or themselves
in the holds of slave ships
the breaking of black males began

| the first breaking

many of the diagrams are wrong
we were not stowed so neatly
limbs overlapping
hallowed hearts
hollow cheeks
mouths tasted
blood
waste
tears
that was the arrangement
our tortured placement

| feet to mouths & tears

you were
young
mother knew
she sang lullabies when the sky was dark
father knew
there was still much for you to learn
your captors knew
but they did not care
they wanted
strong arms and legs
proud backs
but
you were
young

| the children

when i walked through the doorway
looked out the sea
i heard my ancestors call out to me
sorrow awaits when you cross the threshold
a future of bondage
generations sold
high bidders for black bodies
live across the sea
no peace until death
no matter how much you plea

| door of no return

all bodies were not still
spirits defeated
we'd rather die
black skin
ivory bones
between sharks' teeth
we met death
smiling
at our own hands
and do not forgot
there were times
we did not die
alone

| rebellion

run
chains cutting
flesh burning
bloody wounds
keep running
those who do not know what awaits
a new world
they are screaming for you
at you
run
through pale hands grabbing
ignore your captors' voices
listen to your brothers
and sisters
run
jump
let salt water burn your wounds
may the waves pull you under
a quick death
lest you suffer
years and years

| run, jump

ocean
you are the gateway to visit my ancestors
to touch their bones
buried in graves of sand and salt

| mourning at sea continues

i remember
bright colors
fragrant flowers
meals cooking
laughter
singing
dancing
prayer
they cannot take memories
history
truth
i will remember
tell my children
we were not always slaves

| remember

BONDAGE

what makes one man think he can own other
even God does not have this power

| ownership and free will

Every day, hate cracked the air and split the skin on the backs of slaves. It grew in puffs of cotton and hid among the tall stalks of sugar cane.

| from *The Truth About Awiti*

same age
same height
my skin brown
yo' skin white
we was friends
'till i turned three
then i served you
and you owned me

| childhood

love was there
when rape took my virtue
afterward
dark arms
held me close
sweet kisses
took away tears
at night
we whispered
we loved
we prayed
i pushed
birthed
our child
black skin, black curls
proof

| our love

if but for a moment
you were
still born
descending from the heavens
leaving the safety of my warm womb
you saw this sad world
and changed your mind

| clairvoyant stillborn

when i heard men say
don't let slaves read
i knew books was something
that i'd need
all those pages
those words i see
must hold the secrets
to set me free

| education

the slave advertisement warned
she's a runaway by design
gone, honey
i know
you kept running
fighting
i know
they never tamed you

| she gone

in the south
i question branches on trees
did you once hang black bodies
hear victims scream
please
most times i run
unable to walk
i'm too afraid
the trees might talk

| branches & secrets

do you know what it felt like
to walk proud
tell that man
who thought himself our master
i'm back
for my woman
my children
take these coins and paper currency
there is no value in money
only love

|we own us

you were not sent here to be free
so why do you continue to ask
stop your pleas for emancipation

| take it

FREEDOM OR
SOMETHING LIKE IT

i submit
saliva
blood
genealogists provide
percentages of my ancestors' hearts

| this does not make me happy

had you been birthed from another womb
you too
might be
poor
hood
niggerish
who are you to judge
you were
one womb away
from sorrow

| have compassion

some people say
i would have never been a slave
really
because your ancestors are watching you
live in bondage

| what owns you

when we meet
i will run to you and ask
remember the children you wanted to kill
rather than let slavery take them
but love would not let you
i am a woman
born from pain
you let live

| reunited

have you ever wondered
why the ocean calls out to you
many of your ancestors
were not from villages by the sea
salt water
comprised of dark tears
close your eyes
listen to calming whispers
as waves reach your feet
step into their home
welcome gentle currents
stroking your ankles
measuring your waist
eager to embrace
fulfilled hopes and dreams
let your ancestors
love you

| waves

do you see
things can change with just one birth
your mother did not own herself
you told my mother to stay inside
lest the sun darken her skin
i stood in front of mirrors
a towel on my head
singing
pretending my hair was long and blonde
now
my daughter
cocoa skin dances in the sunshine
black locs swing freely
her smile is wide
change is not as slow as we think

| look great grandma, change

i think about what you endured
coast to coast
shore to shore
whips and chains
broken dreams
no justice for black folks
or so it seems
i clench my fists
my chest gets tight
i find it hard to sleep at night
it ain't fair
it just ain't right
that even now
we still must fight

| waiting on justice

there are many ways to resist
one size does not fit all
but each act of defiance
whether silent appeal or loud activism
help

| the struggle

looks like the revolution will be televised
matter of fact
it's already started

| press record | press play

watching the news
reporters speak
of weather and traffic
updates on the week

watching the news
reporters speak
of gunshots and murder
updates on the weak

| live from the scene

close-knit
kin
connected
mourning
each death
every life
taken
unjustly
is personal

| they were ours

black lives mattered
once
when dark fingers picked cotton
and negro breasts nourished white babies
we mattered
worth a fair price
promises of a bounty
if returned unharmed
men argued
hired legal counsel
made certain
they received
full value
then
we became
free
emancipated
valueless

| thoughts on black lives matter

ancestors
when warm raindrops fall
are those your tears
can you believe
we still die such deaths

| murder

i woke up happy
left my home with a smile
hate and more hate
mile after mile
i tried to be kind
pleasantries i supplied
but damn
i was tired
by the time i arrived

| good morning

i've sat with slave owners' descendants
whose parents marched
learned in segregated schools
i've been to their houses
you know
the community that's diverse
neighbors with equal incomes
not equal rights
friends
claiming
they don't see race
and i want to believe them
i really do
but
i can't

| you see it

what can i wear
what can i say
to make sure i don't die today

| living while black

what do you think happened
to the bones of the dead
when thick ropes 'round black necks
separated bodies from heads
flesh burned
ashes danced in the air
settled in the earth
gave birth to despair
wherever you walk
trees and flowers you see
hold remnants of slavery
'twas the death of me

| the south

looks nice, right
melanin
afros and box braids
thick lips, wide hips
these thighs, this ass
blackness
but
do you see
my struggle

|i am not a trend

there are days
i say
let sadness consume my heart
eat my dreams
swallow hope
then i remember
you already died
so that i might live

| depression

words
run across my heart
i remain quiet
trying to catch the truth
before it escapes
my lips

| silence

my writing will always speak to
black people
black history
black stories
black dreams
black truths
black issues
black lives
black deaths
black struggles
blackness
blackity black
black

| writing while black

some readers don't like how words feel
when the truth reaches their souls
many want false redemption
i will not blur the lines
nor taint a sordid history
my writing will hurt

| necessary work

dear ancestors
you survived
you live
on my full lips
in the bend of my curls
reflecting in the melanin dancing on my skin
within the words i write
speak
your tears are my tears
for our past and present
whenever i breathe
i give thanks to you

| dear ancestors

many believe
ancestors whisper in the ears of storytellers
i listen closely
i know
you are guiding me
you've been waiting
for me
to tell your stories

| i believe

ABOUT THE AUTHOR

CHRISTINE PLATT WAS born in 1976 in West Palm Beach, Florida. After graduating from Suncoast Community High School in 1994, she obtained a B.A. in Africana Studies from the University of South Florida, M.A. in African Studies from The Ohio State University, and J.D. from Stetson University College of Law. She began writing under the moniker CP Patrick after marrying her husband, Joseph Patrick, in 2010. CP Patrick enjoys writing fiction and fantasy interwoven with the African diasporic experience. She is the author of the award-winning novel, *The Truth About Awiti*. *Dear Ancestors* is her first collection of poetry.

Visit www.cppatrick.com for additional information.

38611544R00048

Made in the USA
San Bernardino, CA
09 September 2016